Please return/renew this item by the last date shown. Books may also be renewed by phone or internet.

💻 www.rbwm.gov.uk/home/leisure-and-culture/libraries

☎ 01628 796969 (library hours)

☎ 0303 123 0035 (24 hours)

# FEARSOME
# FATS

Written by
John Wood

## BookLife
### PUBLISHING

©2021
BookLife Publishing Ltd.
King's Lynn
Norfolk PE30 4LS

All rights reserved.
Printed in Malta.

A catalogue record for
this book is available from
the British Library.

ISBN: 978-1-83927-484-8

Written by:
John Wood

Edited by:
William Anthony

Designed by:
Jasmine Pointer

## PHOTO CREDITS

*All images are courtesy of Shutterstock.com,
unless otherwise specified. With thanks to Getty
Images, Thinkstock Photo and iStockphoto.*

Scientist character throughout – Designbypex.
Cover – Africa Studio, Nataly Studio, Philip Kinsey. 4–5
– monticello. 6–7 – FotoDuets, KOBRYN TARAS. 8–9
– iprachenko, decoplus, inewsfoto, Andrey_Zakharov.
10–11 – Yuganov Konstantin. 12–13 – New Africa,
Krasula, Zdan Ivan. 14–15 – Krasula, GOLFX. 16–17
– Marian Weyo, DenisProduction.com. 18–19 –
Elena Veselova, DenisProduction.com. 20–21
– Vladimir A Veljanovski, Lightspring. 22–23
– aperturesound, margouillat photo,
Sebastian Duda, New Africa, ifong.

# CONTENTS

Words that look like this can be found in the glossary on page 24.

# A SLICE OF SCIENCE

Are you always being told you shouldn't eat more ice cream? Do you get told to eat more green vegetables? You might be wondering: why does it matter what I eat?

Hello!
I'm a small scientist.
I'm here to teach you about food. Food is very important!

You might have heard the words 'healthy diet'. A diet is the kinds of food you usually eat. To have a healthy diet, you need to make sure you eat the right amount of different food.

A healthy diet is often called a balanced diet because you eat lots of different types of food.

# PORTIONS

A portion of food is the right amount you should eat in one sitting. Sometimes portions are <u>measured</u> in grams.

You can use a scale like this to find out the right portion size in grams.

A portion might be one satsuma.

The right portion size is different for every food. You should have five portions of fruit and vegetables a day. A portion of fruit is roughly the amount you can fit in the palm of your hand.

# WHAT ARE FATS?

Fat is found in lots of food. We only need a small amount of it. Eating too much fatty food can be bad for us.

Let's have a look at some food full of good, healthy fat.

Tofu

Peanut butter

Boiled soybeans

Eggs

# LET'S EXPERIMENT!

This mood bar will tell us about people's bodies. There are four things — how tired they are, how healthy their skin is, how much they can <u>concentrate</u> and how well they can see in <u>dim</u> light.

**ENERGY**

**SKIN**

**CONCENTRATION**

**EYESIGHT**

# WAKE UP

She should eat some nuts. Let's try some almond nuts and Brazil nuts – they have plenty of fat in them. Your body uses fat as extra <u>energy</u>.

Brazil nuts

Almonds

Let's have a look at our second child. The mood bar shows he can't see very well in dim light. I have just the thing...

| ENERGY | SKIN |
|---|---|
| CONCENTRATION | EYESIGHT |

13

# SEEING CLEARLY

Avocado

Give him avocado. Avocado is full of good, healthy fat. Fat helps the body take in <u>vitamins</u> including vitamin A, which helps you see in dim light.

# THE FATS OF LIFE

Feed her fatty fish at once. The fat found in fish helps keep your skin healthy. It is also good for your heart and helps your blood to clot.

Salmon is a type of fish that is full of these healthy fats.

# RISE AND SHINE

Wholegrain cereal

Wait – fat is bad for concentration! Take away this boy's fatty foods. Give him a breakfast of <u>wholegrain</u> cereal. This has vitamin B12, which is good for the brain. It will also give him energy.

ENERGY

SKIN

CONCENTRATION

EYESIGHT

19

# FOOD SWAPS

Fatty meat is full of bad fats.

There are different types of fat. Some fat is healthy, but some is unhealthy. We should try and cut down on bad, unhealthy fats.

Food such as pizza, biscuits and doughnuts are also full of unhealthy fat. It is OK to have these as a treat, but it is important to eat lots of healthy food as well.

Here are some foods full of unhealthy fats.
Try to eat less of these and only have them as a treat.

Sausages

Chocolate

Cakes

Butter

# THE MOST IMPORTANT THING

A small amount of the right kind of fat is very good for you. However, don't forget that it is important to eat lots of different types of food. That is what makes a diet healthy and balanced.

Carbs

Fruit and vegetables

Protein

Fats and sugars

low fat milk

Yogurt

Dairy

# GLOSSARY

| | |
|---|---|
| balanced | made up of the right or equal amounts |
| clot | when blood thickens into a clump near a cut or wound so no blood flows out |
| concentrate | to give your attention to something |
| dim | not a lot of light |
| energy | the ability to do something |
| measured | to have found out the exact amount of something using units or systems, such as grams for weight or metres for distance |
| vitamins | things that are found in food, which your body needs to work properly |
| wholegrain | contains the whole of the grain seed and all the nutrients |

# INDEX